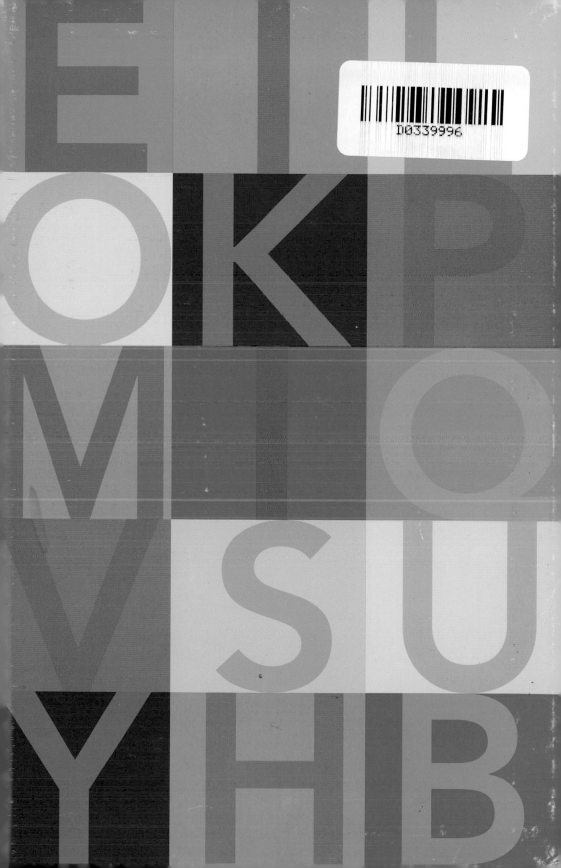

Dear Parents,

Is your child a new reader? If yes, one good way to help your child build confidence and word recognition skills is by introducing word families.

The die-cuts at the bottoms of the pages draw attention to three different word families (letters show through each die-cut shape).

Once your child can read "**ig**", then he or she can focus on the beginning letters and sounds:

pig, wig, dig, jig

After the single words are learned, the pictures help your child read the words in phrases:

pig jig   **pig in a wig**
pig wig   **dig in a wig**

It's much easier to learn a group of words than to memorize them by sight one word at a time. A sight vocabulary is limited by the number of words that can be held in memory.

Recognizing words by families hugely increases the number of words that your child can know. It gives your child a way to sound out new words (reading specialists call these "word attack" skills), thereby increasing the likelihood he or she will feel successful.

Help your child with the 25 new words in this book by giving him or her multiple chances to read it until all the words are mastered.

Most important, have fun together!

Harriet Ziefert, M.A.
Language Arts/Reading Specialist

Pig Wig

by **Harriet Ziefert**

Illustrated by **Yukiko Kido**

flip-a

WORD

Word Families

The world is full of print. Written words are everywhere. It's impossible to learn printed words by memorizing them word, by word, by word. To make learning easier, words can be grouped into families.

The words in a word family have two or more letters that are the same. We read "at" words and "op" words, "it" words and "ug" words. If you know "at," then it's easier to learn bat, hat, and rat.

This book has words from three different word families. All the words in a family rhyme—which means you can add other words to the group by changing the first letter.

It's okay if some of the words you think of are not *real* words. If you make "dat" or "wat" or "lat," it's not wrong— as long as you know the difference between a real word and a nonsense word.

Flip each page and presto-change-o— a new word appears!

The

ig

Family

c
n
k
m
g
p
h
r
d
s
w

pig

j

dig

pig jig

pig wig

Pig, jig in a wig.

Pig, dig in a wig.

The ug Family

f
l
w
m
g
n
b
r
d
w
t

mug

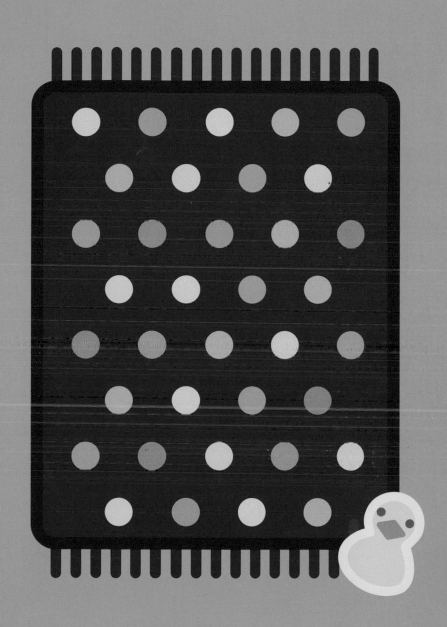

r

bug

mug on a rug

bug and mug on a rug

hug on a rug

bug in mug on a rug

The

at

Family

f
l
w
m
g
n
b
r
d
w
t

cat

b

h

r a t

hat on cat

rat on hat on cat

bat and rat on hat

cat, rat, bat in hat

The ig Family

pig	dig
jig	fig
wig	twig

The ug Family

mug	bug
rug	jug
hug	tug

The at Family

cat	sat
hat	mat
rat	fat
bat	flat

Find the words in each family.

sat cat hat fig wig

rat twig tug dig fat

jig mug sat

jug mug rat dig bug

fig rug jug bat

pig flat twig

hug rug fat tug

dig bug bat hug

hat mat pig flat

cat wig bug tug

mat jig

Word Family Activities

- Choose two words from the word family and make your own "flip-a-word" illustrations. Remember to make a cut-out at the bottom of the page where the word family shows through.

- Words in a word family rhyme. Learn a song or a poem that rhymes and share it. Or read a book that rhymes and guess which words rhyme.

- Write or tell or draw a story using two or three of the characters in this book. What happens next?